Thank you for investing in Volume 1 of

TRENDS *in Offensive Football*

Each season, I spend countless hours studying game film to find the top designs in Offensive Football. Your support of projects like this allow me to continue doing this work. I can't even begin to tell you how much I appreciate it.

Every morning at 5:29am CST I send out a **"One Play a Day"** email to thousands of Coaches & Educated Fans. If you enjoy this project, you can join here:

COACHDANCASEY·COM

Wise old coaches will tell you that football is cyclical. What goes around always seems to come back around.

Who knew the Single Wing would see a resurgence in 2023—nearly a century after it's heyday. Offenses and Defenses are constantly responding to changes in Strategy and Personnel. What works one season, might get figured out by the next season.

Wise old coaches will also tell you that football is fundamentally a copycat game. Just like Picasso said, "Good artists borrow, great artists steal." Since no one owns the patent on GT Counter, we'll just say imitation is the sincerest form of flattery. If you find something in these pages that will work for your team, make sure you put it to good use.

Trends in Offensive Football is designed to help football coaches respond to the most unique and effective schemes from the previous season. The purpose of this book is not to encourage you to follow every trend. You don't need a brand new system, but you might need a few tweaks and wrinkles that keep your team operating at peak efficiency.

If you're a Defensive Coach who stumbled upon this book, hopefully these Trends will inspire you to respond with a creative defensive solution. The most fun I've ever had coaching football is facing a well prepared Defensive Coordinator. Strategic sparing matches sharpen both sides of the ball and keep this great game moving forward.

TRENDS *in Offensive Football*

RUN GAME

Montana State - Quads QB Split Zone

DRAW IT UP

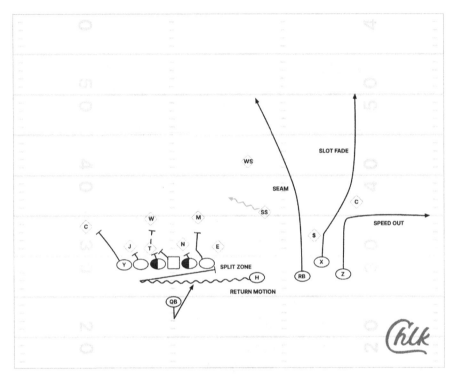

2023 Montana State - Nub Empty Quad Rt H Return QB Split Zone

TAKE NOTES

TRENDS *in Offensive Football*

BREAK IT DOWN

Over the past few seasons, Montana State has assembled one of the most dynamic offenses in all of FCS. They owe much of that success to the two-headed monster at Quarterback of Tommy Mellott and Sean Chambers both of which are dangerous runners. This season they started implementing QB Split Zone out of Empty. They spread the defense by Formation, but still have access to a downhill running game. Here they line up in Empty Nub Quads. They use an H-Back Return Motion to kickout the EMOL (End Man on the Line of Scrimmage) on Split Zone. The Secondary struggles to fit the additional gap and Sean Chambers scampers 68 yards for a Touchdown. This is a fairly simple install for both College and High School teams. In short yardage situations, you can spread the defense out in Empty and take advantage of a lighter box by motioning into QB Split Zone.

CHECK THE TAPE

Category	RUN GAME
Concept	Inside Zone
Play	H Return QB Split Zone

Lions -
Momentum Double Team

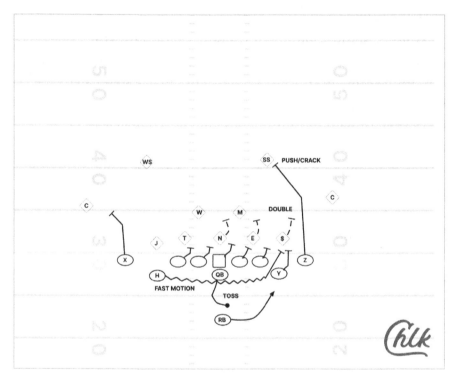

2023 Lions - 12p Ace Rip Toss WZ (Momentum Double)

TAKE NOTES

BREAK IT DOWN

We are experiencing the rebirth of Toss. The 49ers under Kyle Shanahan and the Dolphins under Mike McDaniel have utilized it extensively as part of their base run game. The Detroit Lions have been particularly effective with Toss because of the physicality of their Offensive Line and Tight Ends. They tend to run Toss out of 12 Personnel (1 RB, 2 TE) with a balanced 2x2, "Ace" Formation. They will send the Backside Tight End in Fast Motion across the Formation to Lead the Toss. The TE on the Frontside will engage the Edge Defender and the TE in Motion will bring a late "Momentum" Double Team (almost like a Kick Out Block). Defenders have a difficult time setting the Edge against this Double Team and it allows the play to stretch wider than the typical Toss. It's an Old School Play with a New School Flavor. I expect Offenses to continue iterating on the "Momentum" Double Team.

CHECK THE TAPE

Category	RUN GAME
Concept	Wide Zone
Play	Toss WZ (Momentum Double)

Giants - Wildcat Split Back Bash QB GT Counter

DRAW IT UP

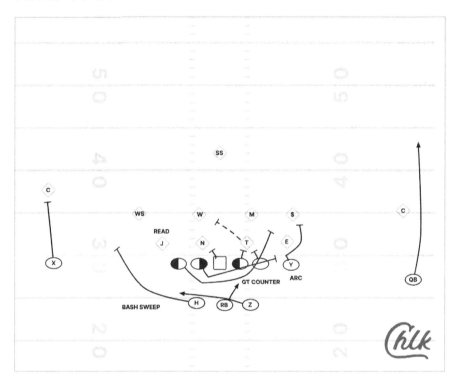

2023 Giants - Wildcat Split Back Bash QB GT Counter

TAKE NOTES

BREAK IT DOWN

The New York Giants were decimated by injuries in 2023. After a promising 2022 season from Daniel Jones, the Giants cycled through 3 different starting quarterbacks and never got their offense on track. In spite of their struggles, I always keep an eye on what their Play Caller Mike Kafka designs each week. While the personnel wasn't there in 2023, the creativity certainly was. One thing the Giants had success with was the Wildcat Formation with Saquon Barkley. Since his time at Penn State with Joe Moorhead, Barkley has always been dynamic with direct snaps. The Giants lined up in Wildcat Split Backs and ran Bash QB GT Counter. The threat of Saquon running Counter was so great that the Lead Bash Sweep turned into an explosive play. While it's difficult to have sustained success at the highest level with Wildcat, these types of plays could certainly benefit High School and College Offenses that need a jumpstart.

CHECK THE TAPE

Category	RUN GAME
Concept	GT Counter
Play	Bash QB GT Counter

Ravens -
Tackle Over Toss Pin & Pull

DRAW IT UP

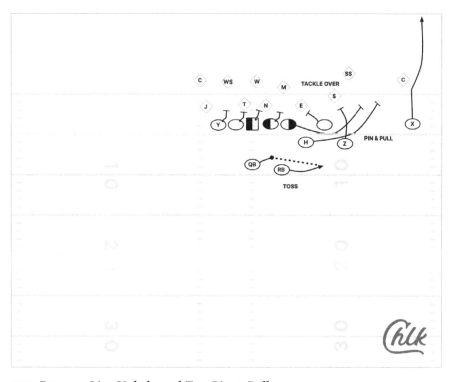

2023 Ravens - Line Unbalanced Toss Pin & Pull

TAKE NOTES

BREAK IT DOWN

John Harbaugh hired Todd Monken to be the Ravens Offensive Coordinator in 2023. The goal was to infuse creativity into their weekly game plan and help QB Lamar Jackson take the next step as a passer. Monken has always been at the cutting edge of Offensive Football with his Screen Designs, but one thing I loved about the Ravens Offense in 2023 was their use of Tackle Over in the Low or Mid Red Zone. Early in the season against Detroit, they used a "Sugar" Huddle and rushed to the line to run Tackle Over Toss Pin & Pull. Later in the season against the 49ers, they use the same "Sugar" Huddle to run Fake toss with a Double Glance + Wheel from the H-Back. What Baltimore did that was truly unique was using a Wide Split for Tackle Over and placing TE/H-Back Isaiah Likely in the Gap. He can either lead on the Toss or run the Wheel - the defense has to decide how they will align to Wide Split.

CHECK THE TAPE

Category	RUN GAME
Concept	Pin & Pull
Play	Unbalanced Toss Pin & Pull

Wisconsin - Motion into Counter

DRAW IT UP

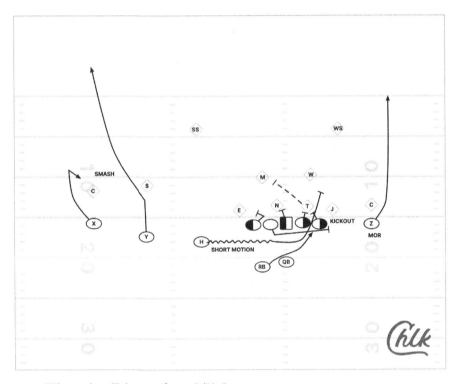

2023 Wisconsin - Trips Lt Short G/H Counter

TAKE NOTES

BREAK IT DOWN

In a move that surprised many in the Big Ten, Phil Longo left North Carolina to join Luke Fickell at Wisconsin. Longo is an Air Raid disciple which seemed out of place at Wisconsin, but his best Offenses at North Carolina ran the ball effectively. Particularly in 2020, Longo fed the two-headed monster of RB Michael Carter and Javonte Williams. Both RB's had over 1,100 yards on the season. Longo may run Air Raid Concepts in the Pass Game, but he attacks with Gap Schemes in the Run Game. One play that Wisconsin ran effectively was G/H Counter, but instead of aligning in 11 Personnel with the H-Back attached to the core, they motioned the H-Back into Counter. This motion can disrupt the "Sniffer" Rules of the defense while allowing the offense to get into a primary Run Scheme. If you use a lot of 10p & 11p you should definitely look into the trend of motioning into Counter!

CHECK THE TAPE

Category	RUN GAME
Concept	G/H Counter
Play	Short G/H Counter

Rams - Duo C-Gap Insert

DRAW IT UP

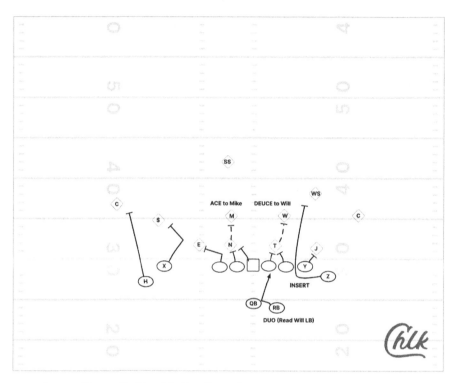

2023 Rams - Deuce Rt Duo (C-Gap Insert)

TAKE NOTES

TRENDS *in Offensive Football*

BREAK IT DOWN

After a challenging 2022 campaign, the LA Rams Offense was reborn in 2023. The most obvious addition was Rookie WR Puka Nacua who was acquired in the 5th Round. Along with Cooper Kupp and a healthy Matthew Stafford, the Rams Pass Game was dynamic. While the Pass Game got publicity, it was the Rams success in the Run Game that really stood out to me. Historically, Sean McVay's best offenses have been able to stay in 10 or 11 Personnel and still run the ball effectively because of how well their WR's block. Guys like Cooper Kupp and Robert Woods gave them Tight End level production in the Run Game from the Wide Receiver position. In 2023, both Kupp and Nacua were heavily involved in the Run Game. One trend that I expect to see explode is how the Rams Inserted their WR into the C-Gap on Duo. A WR who is willing to mix it up in the Run Game is a huge asset in Modern Football!

CHECK THE TAPE

Category	RUN GAME
Concept	Duo
Play	Duo (C-Gap Insert)

UCLA - Slide G-Lead

DRAW IT UP

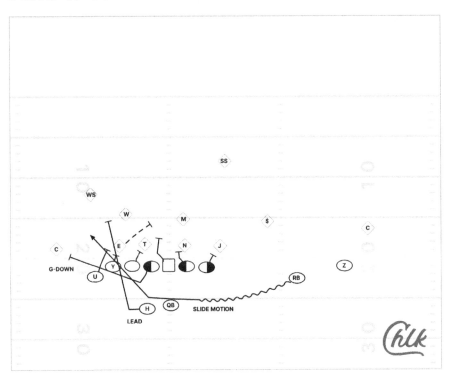

2023 UCLA - TE/Wing Slide G-Lead

TAKE NOTES

TRENDS *in Offensive Football*

BREAK IT DOWN

UCLA had ups and downs in 2023, but Chip Kelly remains one of the best Play Designers in the game. One successful Run Game wrinkle he came up with was a new spin on the classic G-Lead Short Yardage/Goal Line Play. You will often see this play run on the Goal Line out of Jumbo I-Formation. The Frontside Guard will pull to Kickout and the Fullback will Lead inside on the LB. UCLA lined up with TE/Wing into the Boundary and their "Fullback" beside the QB in the typical RB alignment. They used "Slide" Motion to bring the Slot WR into the Backfield. "Slide" Motion starts off like Jet Motion but as the Slot approaches the Tackle Box he will flip his hips and get parallel to the Line of Scrimmage - literally "sliding" next to the QB. Now the elements are in place for G-Lead. The Frontside Guard Kicks, the Fullback Leads and the Slot (in "Slide" Motion) gets the ball. It ended up being an explosive play for the Bruins!

CHECK THE TAPE

Category	RUN GAME
Concept	G-Lead
Play	Slide G-Lead

Sacramento State - Double Wing Counter Criss Cross

DRAW IT UP

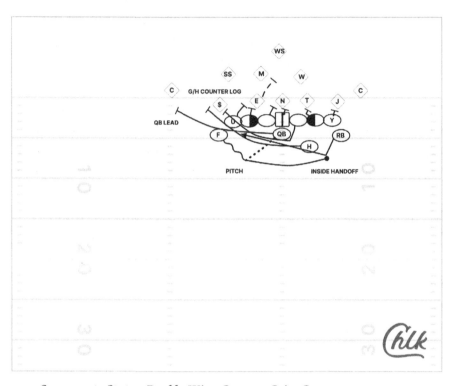

2023 Sacramento State - Double Wing Counter Criss Cross

TAKE NOTES

BREAK IT DOWN

One of my favorite trends in 2023 was the renaissance of Old School Formations in the Red Zone. One of the teams with the most interesting packages was from Sacramento State and their Offensive Line Coach Kris Richardson. They lined up in a Double Wing Formation and ran Counter Criss Cross. The Wing Back shuffles in Motion, takes the Toss (like they are running Sweep or Toss Power). The Wing Back then gives and underneath handoff to the opposite Wing Back. The Guard Pulls to Kick or Log and the Fullback leads on Counter. These Old School plays were highly effective in the Low Red Zone. Sacramento State was able to successfully transform from a Spread Attack to Double Wing when they got in scoring position. Defenses essentially had to prepare for a whole new Offense in the Red Zone.

CHECK THE TAPE

Category	RUN GAME
Concept	G/H Counter
Play	Double Wing Counter Criss Cross

Bixby (OK) - One Man Reverse

DRAW IT UP

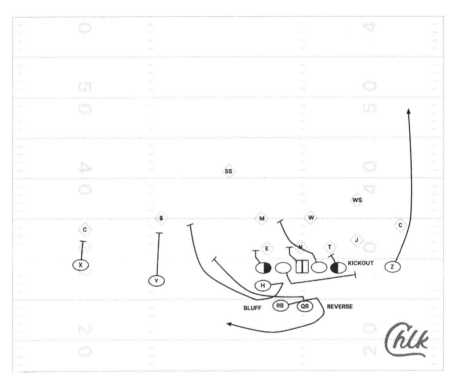

2023 Bixby (OK) - G/H Counter Bluff Reverse (One Man Reverse)

TAKE NOTES

BREAK IT DOWN

Andy Reid famously said that innovation in Offensive Football often trickles up from the lower levels of football. When Kliff Kingsbury was coaching at Texas Tech he wasn't afraid to take a good play design off a recruit's highlight tape. While it's impossible to keep track of all the innovation happening at the High School Level, there are programs like Bixby HS in Oklahoma that are always working on something interesting. Each week, Offensive Coordinator Tyler Schneider finds creative ways to present and package their Base Concepts. This particular play—G/H Counter Bluff Reverse—was massively popular a few years ago, but Bixby added the wrinkle of turning it into a "One Man Reverse." The RB takes the handoff and quickly reverses field to run the reverse all by himself. Andy Reid himself pulled this play out against the Packers from their Wildcat Package. While it wasn't a huge play for the Chiefs, it goes to show you that the best coaches are always experimenting with how they present their Offensive System.

CHECK THE TAPE

Category	RUN GAME
Concept	Reverse
Play	G/H Counter Bluff Reverse

Kansas State - Crunch (Influence/Wham/Trap)

DRAW IT UP

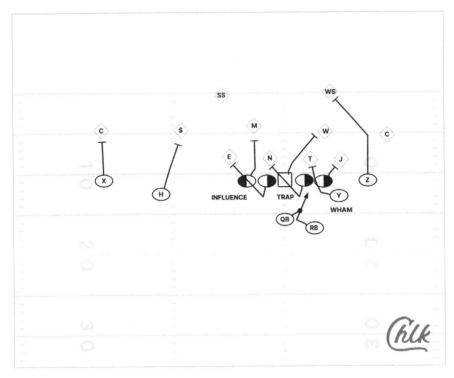

2023 Kansas State - Ace Rt Crunch (Wham Trap)

TAKE NOTES

TRENDS *in Offensive Football*

BREAK IT DOWN

The "Crunch" Play is not new. Some version of Wham/Trap has probably existed since the beginning of football. I know Jim Harbaugh and Greg Roman were running it quite a bit with the 49ers. A lot of Play Callers in both College and the NFL used it this past season against aggressive, penetrating Defensive Lines and I expect to see more of it in the coming years. It is typically run at the 3-Technique (C-Gap Defender). In this clip from Kansas State, the LG pulls to "influence" the LB's. The RG Pulls to Trap the 2i (or Shaded Nose in the A-Gap). The H-Back "Wham" Blocks the 3 Technique. The Center and LT climb up to the Linebackers and the RB is able to get downhill off the Block of the H-Back. Most Linebackers are taught to read the Guards in the Run Game so this is a great way mess with their rules. If Interior Defensive Linemen are pinning their ears back and penetrating, "Crunch" is a great way to slow them down!

CHECK THE TAPE

Category	RUN GAME
Concept	Trap
Play	Crunch (Influence/Wham/Trap)

South Dakota State - Empty Flip C/H Counter

DRAW IT UP

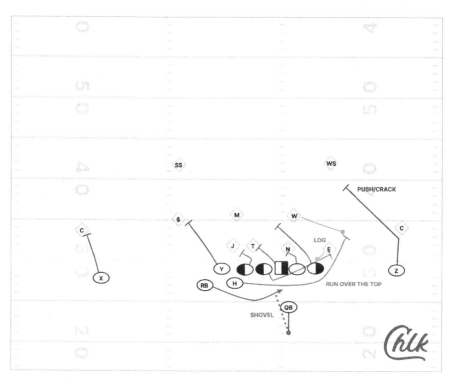

2023 South Dakota State - Empty Quads Bunch Lt Flip C/H Counter

TAKE NOTES

BREAK IT DOWN

In 2023, South Dakota State went 15-0 and won the FCS National Championship. Despite playing in the highly competitive Missouri Valley Conference, their Offense average almost 450 yards per game. Play Caller Zach Lujan parlayed the Jackrabbits success into the Offensive Coordinator job at Northwestern for the 2024 Season. South Dakota State balanced a physical Run Game with creative Formations, Shifts and Motions. On this play they started in a standard Pistol Bunch Formation. Their X Receiver is in the Backfield and their RB is in the Bunch. They motion the WR out into Empty Quads Bunch and they run a Flip C/H Counter to their RB. They are able to run one of their staple plays (C/H Counter) while presenting all sorts of communication challenges to the defense. Getting to Run Schemes out of Empty Bunch is a trend that will show up in more Offenses soon!

CHECK THE TAPE

Category	RUN GAME
Concept	C/H Counter
Play	Quads Bunch Flip C/H Counter

Davidson - False Flow Capped Zone

DRAW IT UP

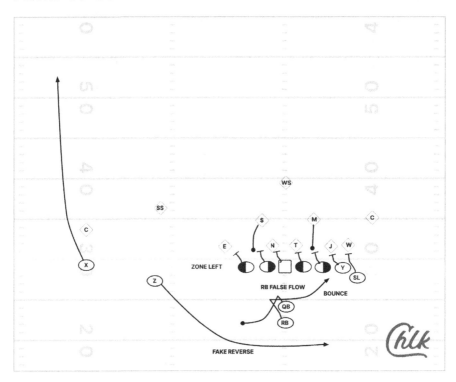

2023 Davidson - TE/Wing Rt False Flow Capped Inside Zone (Fake Reverse)

TAKE NOTES

BREAK IT DOWN

If all you do is study NFL or Power 5 Offenses, you will inevitably miss a lot. There is a ton of variety in the Group of 5 and FCS—I try to do a deep dive on the most efficient offenses each season at every level. Davidson College is consistently one of the top Offenses in FCS Football in recent years. In 2018, Davidson hired Scott Abell from Division-3 Washington & Lee to breathe life into a historically down program. Abell brought a Spread Option attack and has not had a losing season in his 6 years there. They continue to evolve with less Option and more interesting Run Schemes. One thing they implemented last season was what I call a "False Flow" Capped Zone. This simply means that the RB is running against the grain of the Offensive Line. While they are running Zone Schemes, the RB will often bounce to the edge similar to how NFL Offenses use the Duo Scheme. I look forward to seeing the ways Davidson iterates on this moving forward.

CHECK THE TAPE

Category	RUN GAME
Concept	Inside Zone
Play	False Flow Capped Inside Zone

Florida State - Empty Quad QB G/H Counter

DRAW IT UP

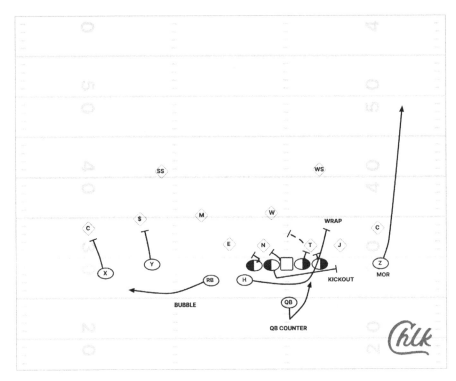

Florida State - Empty Quad QB G/H Counter

TAKE NOTES

TRENDS *in Offensive Football*

BREAK IT DOWN

Empty Quads (4x1) Formations are not common alignments, but they certainly grew in popularity during the 2023 season. Florida State OC and O-Line Coach Alex Atkins is well known for his use of Counter. Over the past several seasons, Florida State has used almost every variation of G/H Counter and GT Counter. They will run Counter with the RB or the QB. One of my favorite Concepts they ran in 2023 was QB G/H Counter out of Empty Quads. They have a Bubble Screen to the Field and QB G/H Counter to the Boundary. This is a great way to stretch the defense horizontally with multiple threats. I personally love running Empty with an H-Back or TE attached. When you have 6 in the Core it opens up the possibility of Gap Schemes (Power & Counter) even out of Empty!

CHECK THE TAPE

Category	RUN GAME
Concept	Inside Zone
Play	Quads QB G/H Counter

Holy Cross - QB G-Lead

DRAW IT UP

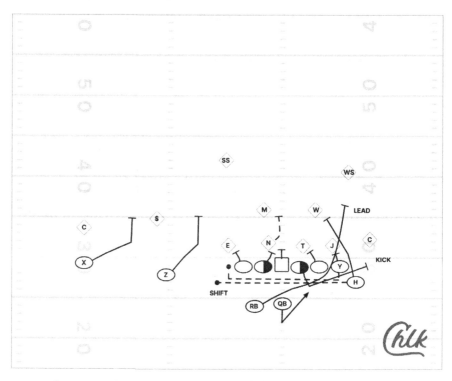

2023 Holy Cross - Shift to TE/Wing Rt QB G-Lead

TAKE NOTES

BREAK IT DOWN

One of the most impressive programs in all of FCS Football has been Holy Cross. Head Coach Bob Chesney took over in 2018 and ended up leading the Crusaders to 5-straight Patriot League titles. In 2024 he was hired by James Madison. Holy Cross had a unique offense that was centered around the skill set of their star QB Matthew Sluka. In back to back season, Sluka rushed for over 1,200 yards. He had the ability to run with physicality between the tackles which meant that Holy Cross almost always had the numbers advantage in the Run Game. One of my favorite plays they ran was a QB G-Lead out of a TE/Wing set. They pull the Frontside Guard to kickout the Edge Defender and the RB Leads on the Quarters Safety. The Quarterback is able to take a gather step and attack downhill. If you are looking for a great way to utilize a physical running QB, I would definitely recommend checking out the Holy Cross Offense!

CHECK THE TAPE

Category	RUN GAME
Concept	G-Lead
Play	QB G-Lead

UCF - Zone Read
with Vertical Relief

DRAW IT UP

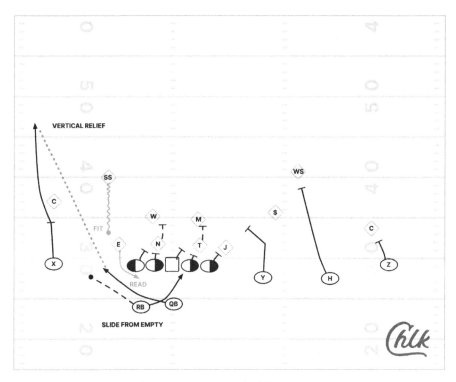

2023 UCF - Empty Rt Slide IZ Read + Vertical Relief

TAKE NOTES

BREAK IT DOWN

When Iowa State faced off with Texas in 2017, Defensive Coordinator John Heacock debuted a 3-Down, 3 Safety Defense that shut down the Longhorns and would go on to beat #3 Oklahoma the very next week. The "Tite" Front (4i-0-4i) would become a major defensive trend in College Football. Because the Defensive Structure lacked a clear "Read" for the QB, the Tite Front forced Offenses away from the QB Zone Read Concept that was popular at the time. We know that scheme is cyclical. Zone Read lost popularity for a few years, but it will come back as Defenses align in more 4-Down or Even Front Structures. Gus Malzahn and UCF started implementing more Zone Read in 2023, but one thing I loved was their Vertical Relief Option. The QB pulls the ball and the Boundary Receiver runs Vertical. If the CB bites to get in the Run Fit, the QB can throw the ball down the field in a way that mimics Triple Option!

CHECK THE TAPE

Category	RUN GAME
Concept	Inside Zone
Play	Zone Read + Vertical Relief

Colts - Goal Line QB Counter

DRAW IT UP

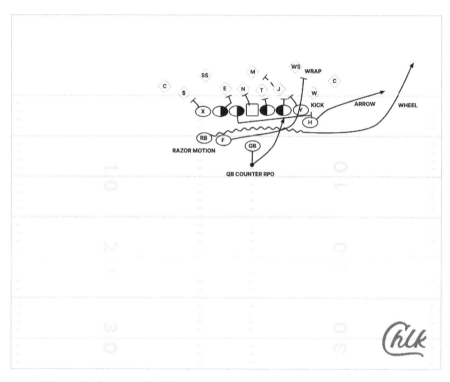

2023 Colts - Shift to Single Wing QB G/H Counter + Arrow RPO

TAKE NOTES

BREAK IT DOWN

One of the most impressive Play Callers in 2023 was Shane Steichen. His ingenuity began with his use of Anthony Richardson and continued after the injury to his rookie phenom Quarterback. Steichen did a great job setting Richardson up with confidence building completions and culminated drives with an impressive arsenal of QB Runs in the Red Zone. One of my favorites was this Goal Line QB Counter RPO. The Colts shifted to a Single Wing Formation with Richardson taking the snap. They fast motion the RB out and run QB G/H Counter to go along with a Wing Arrow Route. If the defense plays slow to the Arrow, Richardson can throw to the Wing. If the Secondary handles the Flat, Richardson can run QB Counter at the Box. Indianapolis scored multiple times on the Counter and also completed the Arrow for a TD. I would expect to see more Low Red Zone designs like this in the coming years!

CHECK THE TAPE

Category	RUN GAME
Concept	G/H Counter
Play	QB G/H Counter + Arrow RPO

Dolphins - Spinner G/H Counter

DRAW IT UP

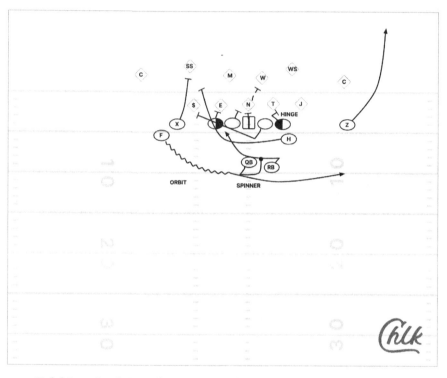

2023 Dolphins - Stack Rt Orbit Spinner G/H Counter

TAKE NOTES

BREAK IT DOWN

I honestly could have filled this entire book with concepts from the Miami Dolphins. Mike McDaniel had a stellar year as a Play Caller. In a copycat league, McDaniel was undoubtedly setting the trends. One of my favorite aspects of the Dolphins play design was their unique Backfield Action. Instead of standard Shotgun handoffs, Tua Tagovailoa would turn his back to the defense for "Spinner" handoffs. This basically allowed Miami to run their Offense from the Shotgun, but still achieve the benefits of operating from Under Center. On this particular play, they motion speedy RB Devon Achane over the top of the QB. Tua fakes the Sweep to Achane and continues spinning to hand G/H Counter to Raheem Mostert. The play itself (G/H Counter) is not revolutionary but the eye-candy is what causes stress for the defense. Orbit Motion over the top is typically telling the defense it's Sweep or Boot, but they also have to account for the underneath handoff on Counter. It's beautiful!

CHECK THE TAPE

Category	RUN GAME
Concept	G/H Counter
Play	Orbit Spinner G/H Counter

0			2
30			30
30			30
40			40
40			40
50			50
50			50
40			40
40			40
30			30
30			30
20			20
20			20
10			10
10			1

TRENDS *in Offensive Football*

SECTION 02

PASS GAME

Dolphins - **Cheetah Dagger**

DRAW IT UP

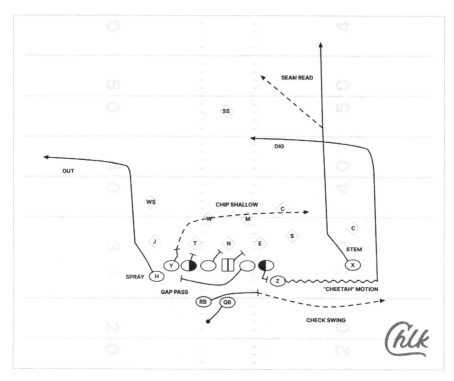

2023 Dolphins - TE/Wing Cheetah Lasso Dagger

TAKE NOTES

TRENDS *in Offensive Football*

BREAK IT DOWN

The Miami Dolphins and Mike McDaniel took the football world by storm in Week 1 with an array of motions and concepts designed to free up Tyreek Hill. I have affectionately called this "Cheetah" Motion as a nod to Hill, but some coaches call it "Exit" Motion or "Escape" Motion. Prior to the snap, the Slot Receiver motions out past the Outside WR at full speed. This causes a frantic switch in coverage responsibilities which has allowed offenses to achieve a leverage advantage. Switch Releases are nothing new, but the speed at which they are occurring on Cheetah Motion is what creates so much difficulty for the defense. McDaniel started using this motion to get Tyreek Hill on the in-breaking Dig Route on their Dagger Concept. He has since used the motion to run Tosses, Screens, Stick and other downfield Passing Concepts. Cheetah Motion quickly became one of the most popular trends in 2023.

CHECK THE TAPE

Category	PASS GAME
Concept	Dagger
Play	Cheetah Lasso Dagger

Packers - Post/Wheel Sail

DRAW IT UP

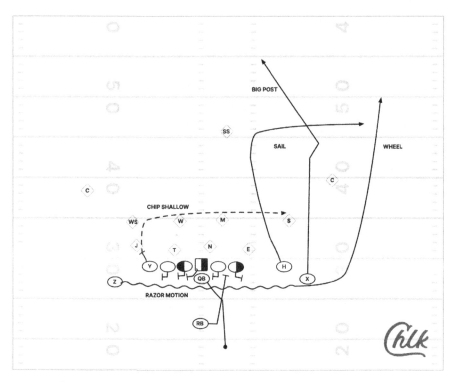

2023 Packers - Ace Razor Post/Wheel + Sail

TAKE NOTES

BREAK IT DOWN

In 2023, Matt LaFleur had the youngest roster in the entire NFL. He was tasked with replacing a Hall of Fame Quarterback in Aaron Rodgers while breaking in a brand new receiving corps for first time starter Jordan Love. The Packers experienced some early season struggles, but as their young WR's matured you could see the Passing Concepts mature with them. By the time they hit the Wild Card round of the Playoffs, LaFleur was dialing up some sinister shot plays off Play Action. On this particular play, the Packers leading WR Jayden Reed motions into a Wheel Route. Speedster Bo Melton is on the Post Route and Romeo Doubs runs a "Sail" Route which looks like a Fake Cross to a Deep Out at 18-20 yards. This is a backbreaking Route Concept for defenses trying to play Single High Safety - versions of Cover 3 or Cover 1.

CHECK THE TAPE

Category	PASS GAME
Concept	Sail
Play	Razor Post/Wheel + Sail

Liberty - **Switch 4 Verts**

DRAW IT UP

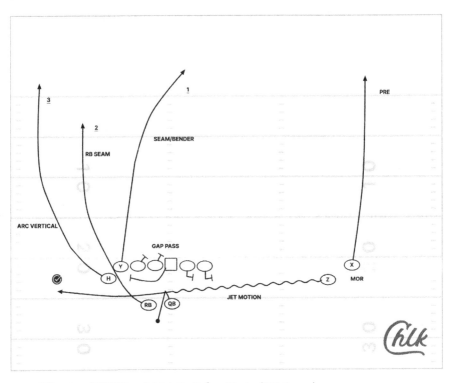

2023 Liberty - TE/Wing Lt Jet Switch 4 Verts (RB Seam)

TAKE NOTES

TRENDS *in Offensive Football*

BREAK IT DOWN

In 2023 Jamey Chadwell took his dynamic Spread Option Offense from Coastal Carolina to Liberty. While Coastal Carolina maintained a strong Option Identity, the 2023 Liberty Offense was a more diverse Spread Attack. One of the most versatile players for Liberty was their Slot WR Aaron Bedgood (#82). While listed as a WR, Bedgood was often used like an Option Slotback spending a good bit of time in the backfield as a blocker or ball carrier. On this particular play, Bedgood is lined up in the Slot and comes in Jet Motion for Power Read. Liberty has TE/Wing aligned into the Boundary. The Wing arc releases on a Vertical, the TE runs the "Bender" Route, and the RB runs the Seam to create the 3x1 spacing in 4 Verts. The trend of getting the RB vertical in the passing game was strong throughout College Football in 2023 and Switch 4 Verts is always hard to stop in the High Red Zone!

CHECK THE TAPE

Category	PASS GAME
Concept	4 Verts
Play	Jet Switch 4 Verts (RB Seam)

Texas - Tempo TE Leak

DRAW IT UP

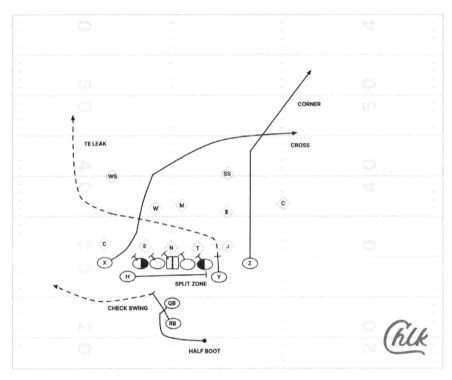

2023 Texas - Pistol Boot TE Leak (Tempo)

TAKE NOTES

BREAK IT DOWN

Few plays got more publicity in 2023 than TE Leak. Obviously it's a concept that has been around for decades, but all levels of football have seen it grow in popularity as Spread Play Caller's find themselves embracing Tight Ends and larger personnel groupings. Every year Texas Head Coach Steve Sarkisian introduces new wrinkles that keep his Offense one of the most efficient in the entire country. One wrinkle he added this season was not only running a lot of TE Leak, but pairing it with Tempo. As Texas got a drive going midway through the 3rd Quarter, the Longhorns raced to the line in 12 Personnel (1 RB, 2 TE). They ran Play Action Split Zone with TE Ja'Tavion Sanders blocking down before working across the formation and drifting vertically on the Leak. It's a difficult play to defend under normal circumstances, but Tempo forced the defense into a more simplified coverage which allowed for an explosive play.

CHECK THE TAPE

Category	PASS GAME
Concept	Leak
Play	Boot TE Leak (Tempo)

Washington - **Middle Screen**

DRAW IT UP

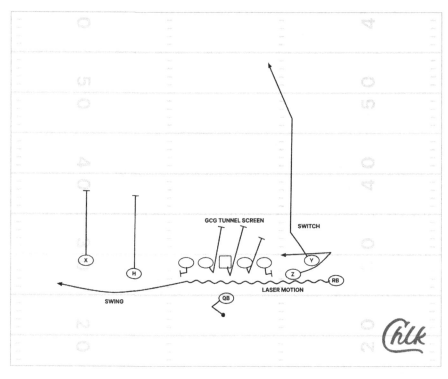

2023 Washington - Empty Bunch Rt Laser Swing + Switch Tunnel

TAKE NOTES

BREAK IT DOWN

The 2023 Washington Huskies had a historic season which culminated in a trip to the College Football Playoff and a chance to play for the National Championship. Head Coach Kalen DeBoer and Play Caller Ryan Grubb constructed one of the most lethal passing attacks in recent memory. In addition to their downfield passing game, Washington utilized a barrage of screens to force defense to tackle their talented receivers in space. Throughout the course of this season, Washington would get into their Pass Concepts out of Condensed Formations with Switch Releases at the Line of Scrimmage. They would use these exact mechanics in their Screen Game which made it difficult to decipher. On this play, they motion out of Bunch and use a Switch Release from #3 to run a Middle or Tunnel Screen. They keep the Tackles in and release Guard, Center, Guard (GCG) on the Screen. They are able to quickly get the ball to one of their most dynamic players.

CHECK THE TAPE

Category	PASS GAME
Concept	Tunnel Screen
Play	Laser Swing + Switch Tunnel

Oregon State - Dash Curl

DRAW IT UP

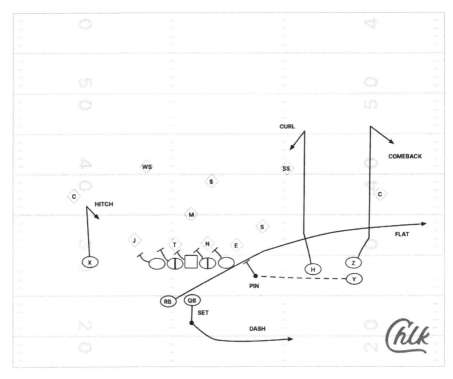

2023 Oregon State - Trips Rt Pin Dash Curl

TAKE NOTES

BREAK IT DOWN

Oregon State's offensive style was unique in the wide open Pac-12. While most teams run Spread, Oregon State Play Caller Brian Lindgren directed a more Pro-Style attack. As a player, Lindgren was a Quarterback at the University of Idaho for longtime NFL O-Line Coach Tom Cable. The West Coast Offense roots are clearly discernible in the 2023 Oregon State Offense. One staple West Coast Concept is "Dash." Think of "Dash" as Boot without Play Action. Some coaches will call it a "Hitch Boot" because the QB peaks at Boundary Quick Game (Hitch or Slant) before escaping to the Field. Oregon State uses the TE to Pin the Edge Defender which allows the QB to break the Pocket. They use a Frontside Curl + Comeback out of 3x1 instead of the traditional Crossing Route from the Backside #2. The Slot Curl finds the soft spot in the Zone against San Diego State's Cover 3 look.

CHECK THE TAPE

Category	PASS GAME
Concept	Dash
Play	Pin Dash Curl

Colorado - Slot Fade Hinge

DRAW IT UP

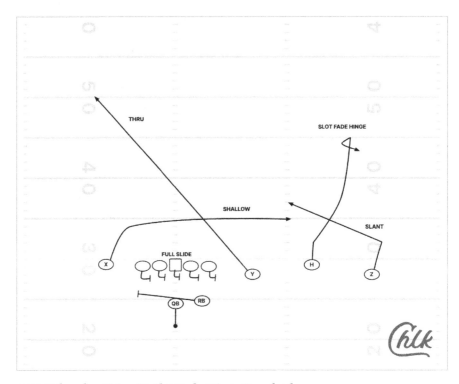

2023 Colorado - Trips Rt Slot Fade Hinge Comeback

TAKE NOTES

BREAK IT DOWN

In 2023, Deion Sanders completely revamped the Colorado Football roster with an influx of talent from his Jackson State squad. With Shedeur Sanders at QB and Travis Hunter playing both ways as a CB and WR, the Buffs shocked the College Football world with an upset of National Champion runner-up TCU. Play Caller Sean Lewis brought an uptempo approach that paired well with the new offensive talent early in the season. One concept that Colorado thrived on was the Slot Fade. Out of a 3x1 Formation, the #2 Receiver (often Travis Hunter) would run an Inside Slot Fade on either a Safety or a Nickel. His speed, length and ball skills made this route almost unguardable by opposing defenders. As TCU adjusted to the Slot Fade by playing with more depth, Colorado was able to convert the Slot Fade into a "Hinge" Comeback Route. As the Slot Fade continues in popularity, this "Hinge" Comeback will certainly be a trend to keep an eye on.

CHECK THE TAPE

Category	PASS GAME
Concept	Slot Fade
Play	Slot Fade Hinge Comeback

Missouri - **Bunch to Boot**

DRAW IT UP

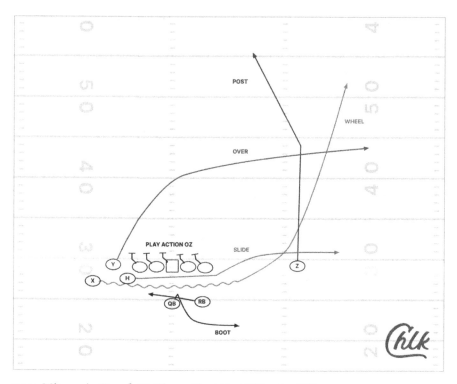

2023 Missouri - Bunch Lt Blazer Boot Post/Wheel + Slide

TAKE NOTES

BREAK IT DOWN

In 2023 Missouri experienced a breakout season under new Offensive Coordinator Kirby Moore. One of the greatest strengths of their Offensive System was the way they packaged plays and worked in "Sequences." The idea of Sequencing Plays is a foundational philosophy of the Wing-T. While Mizzou doesn't run the Wing-T, you can see the ways their concepts build off one another. One of their most effective concepts was out of FIB Boundary Bunch (FIB = Formation into the Boundary). From the Bunch, #1 would motion across the formation into a Wheel Route. The #3 WR in the Bunch would often be their best Offensive Playmaker Luther Burden who would run the Post Snap "Slide" Route into the Flat. The QB would Boot with the ability to throw the Wheel, throw the Slide or run himself. They would often use the same action and hand the ball off to the RB. I expect to see this Sequence and more like it in 2024!

CHECK THE TAPE

Category	PASS GAME
Concept	Boot Slide
Play	Blazer Boot Post/Wheel + Slide

Ole Miss - Switch Y-Cross

DRAW IT UP

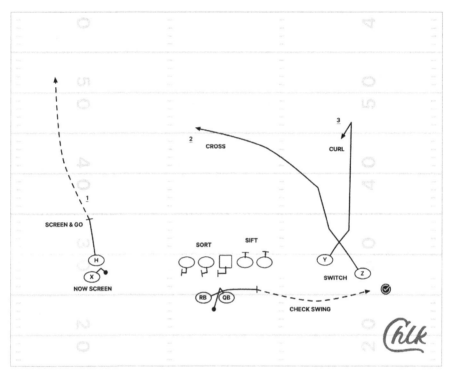

2023 Ole Miss - Ace Lt Stack Switch Y-Cross (+ Screen & Go)

TAKE NOTES

BREAK IT DOWN

You could look at any football season from the past 20 years and Y-Cross could be considered a "trend" because everyone is runs it. At this point, it's not so much what you run, but how you run it. Lane Kiffin and Charlie Weis Jr. have continued to expand the ways in which they get to their base concept of Y-Cross. On this particular play they are using a Frontside Screen & Go paired with a Backside Switch Release. The spacing remains almost identical to their base version of Y-Cross, but it presents differently to the defense. Most impressively, the are often running concepts like this off Tempo. They are able to deliver complexity at a high rate of speed - that makes life tough for the Defense. This is further proof that you don't need to reinvent the wheel. Run staple concepts like Y-Cross or Mesh, but present them in a creative way.

CHECK THE TAPE

Category	PASS GAME
Concept	Y-Cross
Play	Switch Y-Cross + Screen & Go

Colts - Empty Orbit Mesh

DRAW IT UP

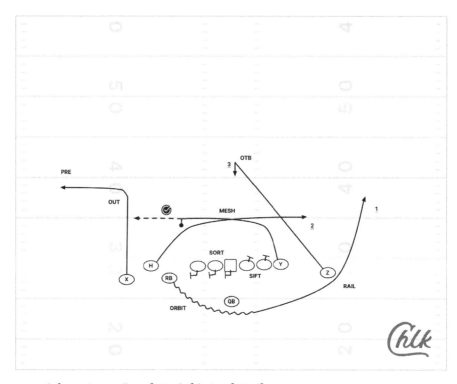

2023 Colts - Empty Bunch Lt Orbit Mesh Rail

TAKE NOTES

TRENDS *in Offensive Football*

BREAK IT DOWN

In the Spring of 2022, I published "The Ultimate Guide to Mesh." It was my 300+ page manifesto on the Mesh Concept and the various ways it can be implemented in any Offensive System. Mesh obviously wasn't new in 2022 and it certainly isn't new in 2023, but the ways coaches are getting to Mesh continue to evolve. Shane Steichen used the Concept quite a bit with the Colts in 2023, but one of my favorite ways he ran it was out of Empty Bunch. The Colts used Orbit Motion to get across the Formation to the Rail Route. The typical progression for the Quarterback is Rail, Shallow, Sit (OTB). What I have noticed is that defenses are quick to take away initial reads on Mesh Rail now that they see it so often. The Quarterbacks who are able to work all the way back to the other Shallow on the Backside of Mesh tend to find a lot of completions.

CHECK THE TAPE

Category	PASS GAME
Concept	Mesh
Play	Orbit Mesh Rail

Kentucky - Leak with RB Wheel

DRAW IT UP

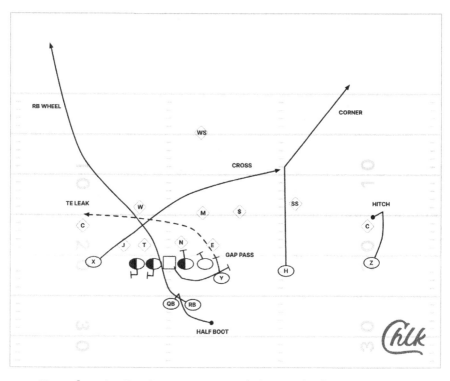

2023 Kentucky - Ace Rt Rip Power Pass Leak (+ RB Wheel)

TAKE NOTES

BREAK IT DOWN

One of the most popular plays in 2023 was TE Leak. Kentucky OC Liam Coen had brought a Pro-Style identity with him from the NFL to Lexington, KY. While the TE Leak is a Concept that is often associated with West Coast or Pro-Style Offenses, it has started showing up more consistently in Spread Offenses as well. One wrinkle that Coen and others have experimented with is the use of the Play Action RB Wheel in addition to Leak. Essentially the RB fakes the handoff and works through the Line of Scrimmage on a Wheel Route. The Quarterback works High to Low off Boot Action: RB Wheel to TE Leak. If the RB breaks free it's a chance for an explosive play, if the underneath Zone Defender carries the Wheel, the Leak will replace the open space. Look for Play Callers to continue evolving the TE Leak in 2024 and beyond!

CHECK THE TAPE

Category	PASS GAME
Concept	Leak
Play	Power Pass Leak (+ RB Wheel)

Seahawks - TE Delay

DRAW IT UP

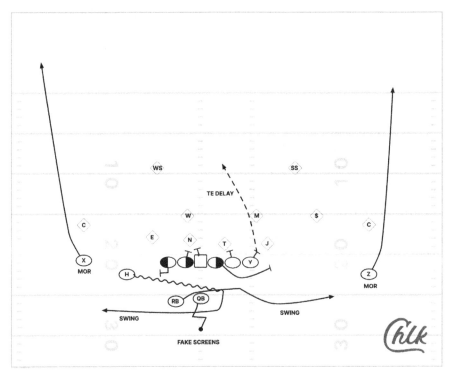

2023 Seahawks - Deuce Rt Return Double Screen + TE Delay

TAKE NOTES

BREAK IT DOWN

I recently joked that every branch of Kyle Shanahan's Tree called this play in 2023. It's certainly not a new concept, but it exploded in popularity this past season. It has its own section in *The Ultimate Guide to Screen*. The first time I saw it show up on film was Bill Walsh's West Coast Offense. The premise of the play is to fake a Swing Screen to the Boundary, fake a Swing Screen to the Field and finally throw the Delayed Seam to the TE over the middle of the field. The goal is to use all that action to get the Linebackers and Safeties to split leaving a void in the middle of the field. The creativity on this play is the eye candy used to get the defense moving. I like how the Seahawks used Return Orbit Motion for the first fake screen.

CHECK THE TAPE

Category	PASS GAME
Concept	TE Delay
Play	Double Screen + TE Delay

Montana - Screen & Go Follow

DRAW IT UP

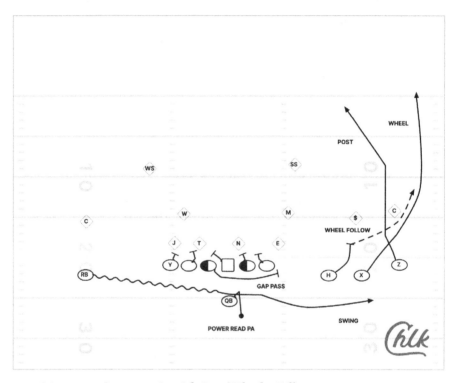

2023 Montana - Screen & Go with Post/Wheel + Follow

TAKE NOTES

BREAK IT DOWN

I often say that if you want some of the best ideas in Offensive Football you need to watch FCS Football. The Football Championship Series (formerly known as Division 1-AA) is played at a very high level. Since it's out of the spotlight of the national media and message board culture you tend to see more variety in Offensive Scheme. You still see teams that run the Triple Option or are willing to think outside the box. Montana plays in the highly competitive Big Sky Conference and they did a great job in 2023 maximizing the skill set of their Quarterback Clifton McDowell. They often used Wide Splits, Empty Formations and Perimeter Screens to spread out the Defense. On this particular play they lined up in Empty, ran Play Action Power Read paired with a Perimeter Screen & Go. The outside WR's run Post/Wheel and #3 runs a Wheel "Follow." If the underneath defender matches the initial Wheel it leaves space for the Follow!

CHECK THE TAPE

Category	PASS GAME
Concept	Screen & Go
Play	Screen & Go with Post/Wheel + Follow

Oregon - Double Post Sail

DRAW IT UP

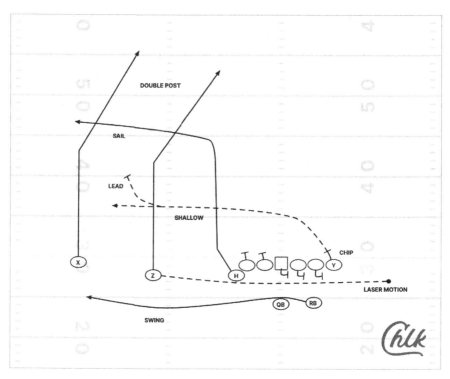

2023 Oregon - Nub Trips Lt PA Double Post Sail (RB Swing)

TAKE NOTES

BREAK IT DOWN

Play Callers love to call "Shot" Plays on the plus side of the 50 yard line. The key is to have a Quarterback with the maturity to check the ball down if you don't get the right look or matchup. You don't always need to throw the Big Post. In 2023, Oregon had a great combination of Quarterback Bo Nix and Play Caller Will Stein. Oregon would often dial up Shot Plays like this because the worst case scenario was a check down for positive yardage instead of a Sack or Interception. The old adage holds true, "you can't go broke making a profit." This play in particular is a mashup of 2023's greatest hits: Sail/Flood with a Double Post + Lead Swing Screen. Oregon essentially gets to a 5-Strong Concept which is nearly impossible for Zone Defenses to match. When the Flat Defender runs underneath the Sail Route, the RB Swing is wide open for an explosive check down!

CHECK THE TAPE

Category	PASS GAME
Concept	4-Strong
Play	Double Post Sail (RB Swing)

Chiefs - Quads Trail Follow

DRAW IT UP

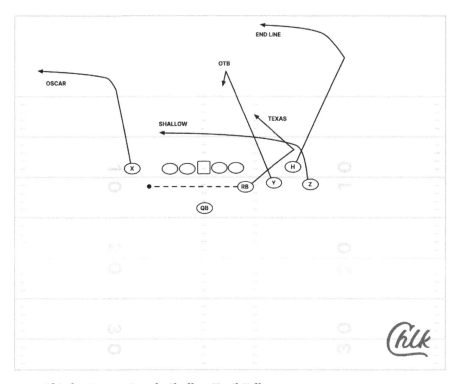

2023 Chiefs - Empty Quads Shallow Trail Follow

TAKE NOTES

BREAK IT DOWN

Andy Reid and the Kansas City Chiefs are constantly challenging defenses in the Red Zone. Some games they line up in Old School Formations that are relics from a forgotten era of football. Some games they line up in Empty and let Patrick Mahomes go to work. A lot of defenses will use Match Coverage Principles in the Red Zone. In other words, they will sort out the switches at the line of scrimmage and quickly match up in Man Coverage. On this play, the Chiefs motion RB Isaiah Pacheco to Quads and run a Shallow Trail/Follow Concept. The Shallow comes from the #1 WR and the Trail (Texas Route) comes from #4. You can see the LB is attempting to out leverage Pacheco into the Flat and instead he breaks back inside on the Texas Route. If you run into Red Zone Match Coverage, this is a great answer for it!

CHECK THE TAPE

Category	PASS GAME
Concept	Shallow Trail
Play	Quads Shallow Trail Follow

South Carolina - G/H Counter Slip Arrow Screen

DRAW IT UP

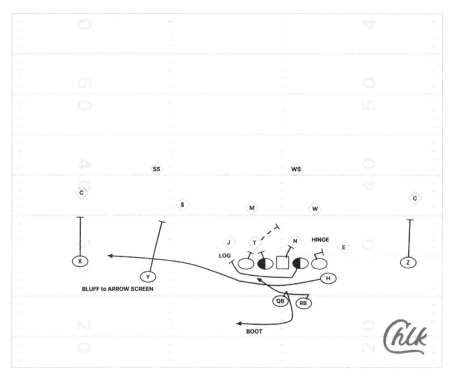

2023 South Carolina - Ace Rt G/H Counter Boot Bluff Arrow Screen

TAKE NOTES

BREAK IT DOWN

G/H Counter is a staple run play in Offenses that operate out of 11p (1 RB + 1 TE or H-Back). There have been several trends building off that initial framework. In the Run Game section, you saw how Bixby (OK) HS ran a "one man reverse" off G/H Counter Bluff Reverse Action. This play from South Carolina is in a similar family. They use G/H Counter action but Slip the H-Back into the Flat on the Arrow Route to set up the Screen. This is particularly effective against defenses that Spill Counter and force the H-Back to run over the top. As long as the ball is caught behind the line of scrimmage, blockers can be engaged with Back 7 Defenders. I expect to see Counter teams use a lot more of these creative Screens, especially if they have a dynamic H-Back!

CHECK THE TAPE

Category	PASS GAME
Concept	Arrow Screen
Play	G/H Counter Boot Bluff Arrow Screen

Dolphins - Lead Swing Screen

DRAW IT UP

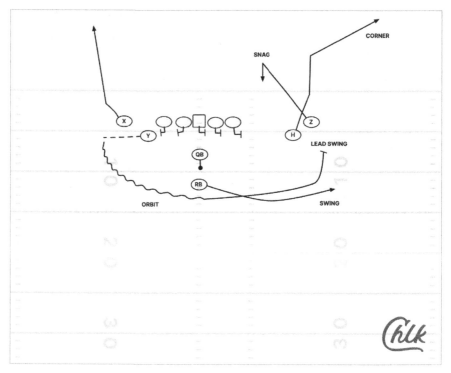

2023 Dolphins - Pistol Ace Lt Cheetah Orbit 4 Strong Snag (Lead Swing)

TAKE NOTES

BREAK IT DOWN

If you are noticing a theme in the Pass Game, it's probably 4-Strong. Play Callers are flooding zones like never before. One powerful addition to the 4-Strong trend is the Lead Swing Screen. Defensive Coaches usually prefer to force the check down and rally to ball to make the tackle for a short gain. Now Offensive Coaches are protecting the Swing check down with a lead blocker. In this clip the Dolphins get 4-Strong in the Red Zone. The TE is able to lead block for the Swing Route and no other defender is able to pursue to the football in time. Throughout the 2023 season you saw the Dolphins, 49ers, Ravens and others use this strategy of 4-Strong with a Lead Swing. It is the perfect mix of the Downfield Passing Game and Perimeter Slow Screens. I would expect this to be a massive trend in the coming seasons until defenses find an answer.

CHECK THE TAPE

Category	PASS GAME
Concept	4-Strong
Play	4-Strong Snag (Lead Swing)

Michigan - RB Mesh Traffic

DRAW IT UP

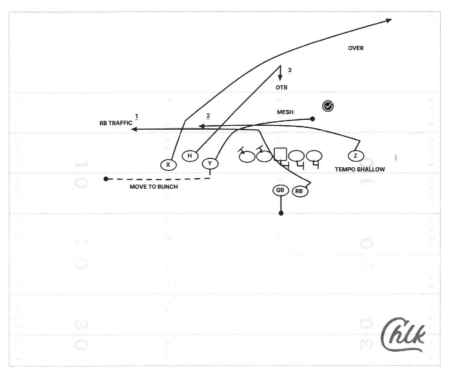

2023 Michigan - MT Bunch Lt RB Mesh Traffic

TAKE NOTES

BREAK IT DOWN

The Running Back position has been devalued in professional football. Due to the toll of a 17 game schedule and the risk of injury, NFL teams are reluctant to invest big money into the position. Coaches, on the other hand, clearly value a Running Back with a diverse skill set, particularly if they can catch the football out of the backfield. Play Callers love to utilize their Running Back in the Low Red Zone. Not only can they hand them the ball, but one of the most effective scoring plays in 2023 was throw the ball to the RB on "Mesh Traffic." In this clip from Michigan, you see Blake Corum escape through the A-Gap to run through the Mesh Concept. He comes wide open for a walk-in Touchdown in one of the most critical drives of Michigan's season. RB Mesh Traffic was a huge trend in 2023. There was a stretch where it seemed like every NFL Offense scored with it. You will see more creative ways to utilize the RB in the Red Zone in years to come!

CHECK THE TAPE

Category	PASS GAME
Concept	Mesh
Play	RB Mesh Traffic

Texas State - FIB Mesh Rail

DRAW IT UP

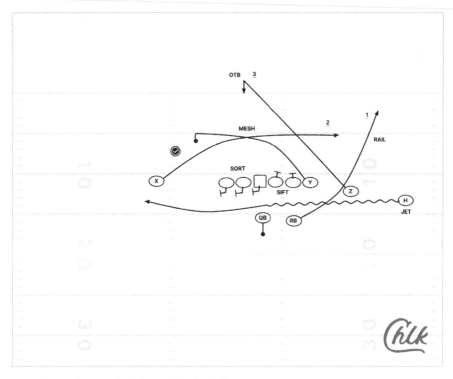

2023 Texas State - FIB Laser Mesh Rail

TAKE NOTES

BREAK IT DOWN

GJ Kinne took over as the Head Coach of Incarnate Word (FCS) in 2022. In his only year in San Antonio, UIW had one of the most explosive Offenses in FCS history. Play Caller Mack Leftwich led an attack that was reminiscent of the Art Briles Baylor Offense. Deep Choice Passing Game and Downhill Run Game. Both Kinne and Leftwich took over at Texas State in 2023 resurrecting a long dormant program. While the Offense still worked to push the ball vertically, they also added some new wrinkles—particularly in the Red Zone. They play with extreme Tempo and they used that tempo to get into FIB (Formation into the Boundary). They motioned #1 to the Field and ran 2x2 Mesh Rail. The RB came free for a walk-in touchdown in their upset of Baylor. Mesh Rail is nothing new, but getting to FIB Mesh Rail with a motion off Tempo can cause a lot of problems for the defense. I like how Texas State translated a complex concept into a "One Word Call."

CHECK THE TAPE

Category	PASS GAME
Concept	Mesh
Play	FIB Mesh Rail

Washington -
4-Strong Sail from the RB

DRAW IT UP

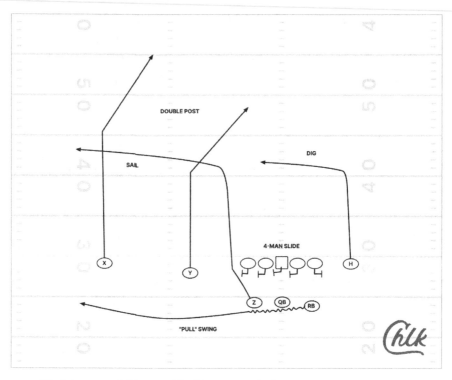

DOUBLE POST

SAIL

DIG

4-MAN SLIDE

X

Y

Z · QB · RB

H

"PULL" SWING

Chlk

2023 Washington - Split Lt Pull Dbl Post RB Sail

TAKE NOTES

BREAK IT DOWN

If there was a theme that ties together the trends in the Passing Game it's 4-Strong. Flooding the Zone has created some of the most profound problems for Defenses in 2023. You already saw Will Stein at Oregon running their 4-Strong Double Post "Flood" Concept. I also wanted to highlight how Washington OC Ryan Grubb got to their 4-Strong Look. You get the same Double Post from Washington, but because they align in Split Backs the Sail Route has to come from the Backfield. Grubb aligned WR Jalen McMillan in the Backfield to run the Deep Out. With Michigan State in a Quarters Coverage Structure, the 4-Strong Flood gets McMillan matched up on the Mike LB. The speed and athleticism is just too much for the Linebacker and Washington gets an easy completion. If the Nickel Sam sank underneath the Sail Route, QB Michael Penix could check the ball down the RB in "Pull" Motion.

CHECK THE TAPE

Category	PASS GAME
Concept	4-Strong
Play	Dbl Post RB Sail

Iowa State - Split Zone Pop Seam

DRAW IT UP

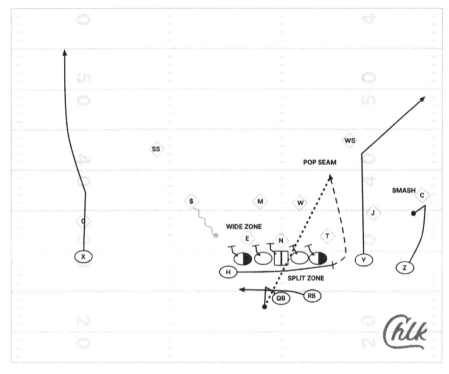

2023 Iowa State - Slant Lt Split Wide Zone Pop Seam

TAKE NOTES

BREAK IT DOWN

Over the past several years, we have seen entire offensive systems built from Split Flow Principles. They will use 11 Personnel with the TE off the ball and run variations of Split Zone and Counter. This is highly effective because it not only allows for a physical run game, but it also sets up a robust Boot & Keeper Series. Most Offenses that use Split Flow will often run "Bluff" Concepts where the QB will read the DE and the H-Back will avoid and lead block for a QB Keep. This is also an effective Boot technique with the H-Back avoiding and working into the flat. Iowa State adds an interesting wrinkle with the H-Back avoiding inside the EDGE player and working Vertical into the Seam. This is a great way to take advantage of defenses that like to jump the flat on Boot.

CHECK THE TAPE

Category	PASS GAME
Concept	Pop Pass
Play	Split Wide Zone Pop Seam

Texans - Filter Screen

DRAW IT UP

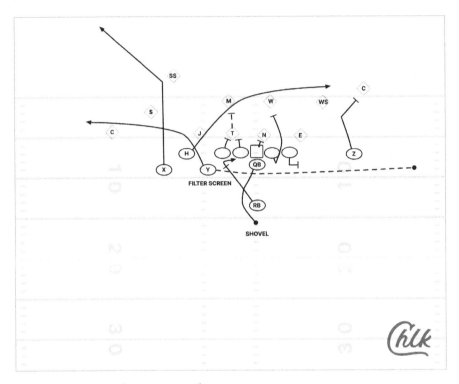

2023 Texans - Bunch Lt PA RB Filter Screen

TAKE NOTES

TRENDS *in Offensive Football*

BREAK IT DOWN

In 2023 the Houston Texans drafted QB C.J. Stroud and hired Bobby Slowik as Offensive Coordinator. Before coming to Houston, Slowik served as the Pass Game Coordinator for Kyle Shanahan in San Francisco. As other franchises continue to hire coaches away from Shanahan, we are seeing similar schemes show up across the league. One play that Shanahan, Mike McDaniel and Slowik all ran was the Red Zone "Filter" Screen. It's a Play Action Concept for the Low Red Zone where the RB attacks the Edge Defender and pivots inside for the Shovel Pass. Most football coaches and fans are familiar with Jon Gruden's "Spider 2 Y-Banana." This is the Screen Variation of Spider 2 Y-Banana. Defenses are quick to cover the Flats leaving the middle Shovel Screen available. The Filter Screen is some Low Red Zone sorcery that keeps defenders honest!

CHECK THE TAPE

Category	PASS GAME
Concept	Filter Screen
Play	PA RB Filter Screen

Texas - Boot RB Throwback Screen

DRAW IT UP

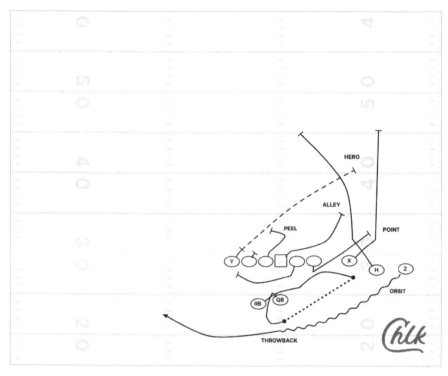

2023 Texas - Nub Trips (FIB) Orbit PA Gap Pass RB Throwback Screen

TAKE NOTES

BREAK IT DOWN

One of the core tenants of a Steve Sarkisian Passing Game is what he calls the "Gap Pass." That means Play Action with a Guard pulling in Protection. Longtime NFL Offensive Coordinator Greg Roman famously said, "It's not Play Action unless you pull a Guard." If you study the Texas Offense you will find a wide variety of "Gap Pass" Play Action Concepts. In addition to their downfield Passing Game, one of the Longhorns' most explosive plays was a Boot RB Throwback Screen with a Pulling Guard. Offensive Line Coach Kyle Flood said this is the concept people ask them about the most. The Quarterback Boots with the Guard and spins back to the RB for the Throwback Screen. Because of the "Gap Pass" Protection, Texas is able to get 3-4 Offensive Linemen out to lead the Screen. I would expect a lot of Play Callers to steal this screen in the coming years!

CHECK THE TAPE

Category	PASS GAME
Concept	Throwback Screen
Play	Gap Pass RB Throwback Screen

TRENDS *in Offensive Football*

SPECIALS

Kansas - Polecat Fly Sweep

DRAW IT UP

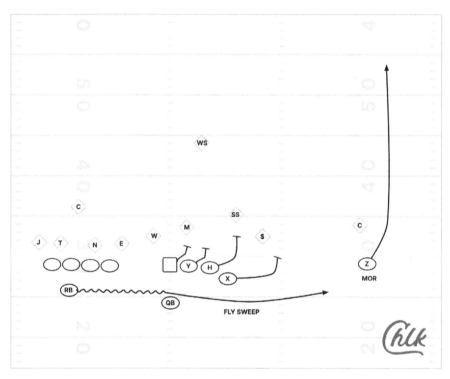

2023 Kansas - Polecat Fly Sweep

TAKE NOTES

TRENDS *in Offensive Football*

BREAK IT DOWN

Kansas Play Caller Andy Kotelnicki is one of the most creative game-planners in all of football. One of his greatest strengths is his use of Pre-Snap Shifts. Kansas will routinely shift to Unbalanced Formations and force the defense to make multiple checks before the ball is ever snapped. Most Defensive Coordinators preach "Alignment, Assignment, Technique." The Pre-Snap Shifts that Kansas uses gets defenders so worried about Alignment and Assignment which causes Technique to falter. Here Kansas shifts into a "Polecat" Formation—a nod to the great Glenn "Tiger" Ellison who is credited with its invention. The entire Offensive Line shifts to the Boundary and Kansas uses Jet Motion to run a Fly Sweep back to the Field. Kotelnicki will generally utilize several Shifts or Odd Formations per game forcing the defense to waste valuable time on the sideline addressing player questions. Pre-Snap Shifts are a hallmark of effective Offenses and you can expect to see more Formations like this.

CHECK THE TAPE

Category	SPECIALS
Concept	Polecat
Play	Polecat Fly Sweep

New Mexico State - Wildcat QB Sprint Out

DRAW IT UP

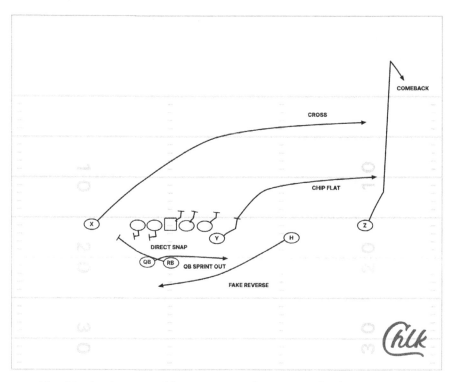

2023 New Mexico State - Wildcat QB WZ Fake Reverse Flood

TAKE NOTES

BREAK IT DOWN

New Mexico State shocked the college football world with a 10-win season. Most surprising of all was their upset victory over Auburn in Jordan-Hare Stadium. A big reason for the success of Aggies was their talented, hard-nosed Quarterback Diego Pavia who was a State Champion Wrestler in High School. Pavia ran for almost 1,000 yards on the ground in 2023 and the threat of him running allowed New Mexico State to be creative with their Wildcat Package in the Red Zone. On more than one occasion they ran this Wildcat QB Sprint Out play for touchdowns. As you can see: the direct snap goes to the Running Back, hand off to the Quarterback, Fake Reverse to the Slot and it finally turns into a Sprint Out/Boot to a Flood Concept with a Stem Corner from the Z, an Over from the X and a Chip to Flat from the H-Back.

CHECK THE TAPE

Category	SPECIALS
Concept	Wildcat Spring Flood
Play	Wildcat QB WZ Fake Reverse Flood

Washington State - 2 QB Boot

DRAW IT UP

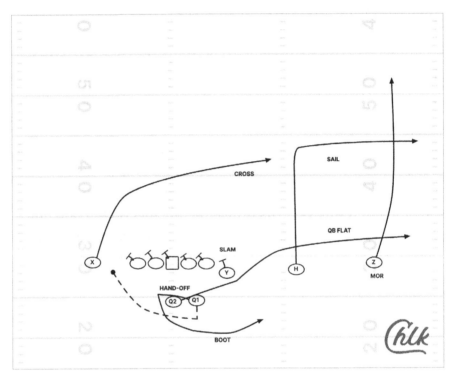

2023 Washington State - Empty to 2-QB Boot to Flood

TAKE NOTES

BREAK IT DOWN

It's about time we talk about one of the most significant Trends in all of Offensive Football. The 2-QB Offense should probably be its own book. I remember first becoming enamored with it when James Perry was the OC at Princeton and he had both a Righty and Lefty QB. The team that has made it most famous recently is Andy Kotelnicki at Kansas with Jalon Daniels and Jason Bean. Washington State Play Caller Ben Arbuckle got in on the action in 2023 and I really liked his version. QB2 takes the snap and hands off to QB1 who quickly reverses field on Boot. Meanwhile QB2 releases into the Flat on the Flood Concept. In both High School and College Football your top 2 Quarterbacks are often some of the better athletes on the roster. This is a great way to get multiple Quarterbacks involved without creating a controversy. While I expect to see an explosion of 2-QB Concepts in HS and College, I've also talked to NFL guys who are looking for ways to implement it. Keep a close eye on this trend!

CHECK THE TAPE

Category	SPECIALS
Concept	2-QB
Play	2-QB Boot to Flood

Chargers - Cross Field Lateral

DRAW IT UP

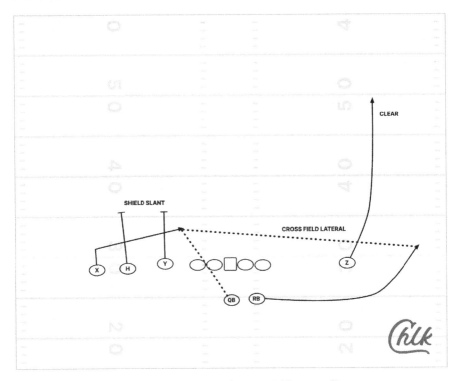

2023 Chargers - Trips Lt Shield Screen (Cross Field Lateral)

TAKE NOTES

BREAK IT DOWN

While 2023 was a tough year for the Chargers, I always keep an eye on the creative designs from Kellen Moore. His Offenses in Dallas were consistently at the top of the league and he always added interesting wrinkles (particularly in the Pass Game). Every once in a while you see a play that makes you jump up out of your seat. This Cross Field Lateral from the Chargers certainly did that for me. On 3rd & Long, you will often get conservative coverage from the defense. One way to combat that is with a Shield Screen followed by a Cross Field Lateral to the RB. I remember first seeing this a few years ago when the New York Jets ran it and I don't understand why this isn't attempted more often. In my mind, the biggest risk is the lateral being thrown out of bounds. I hope Football follows the lead of Rugby and we start seeing more laterals!

CHECK THE TAPE

Category	SPECIALS
Concept	Lateral
Play	Shield Screen (Cross Field Lateral)

William & Mary - Flea Flicker with TE Delay Wheel

DRAW IT UP

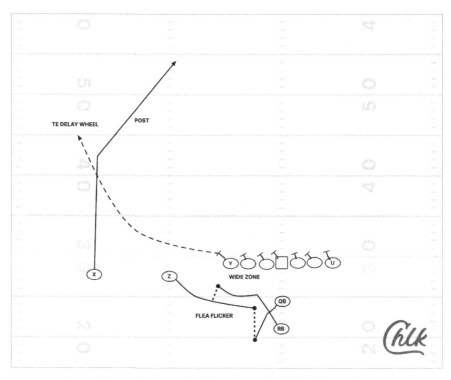

2023 William & Mary - Trey Lt WZ Reverse Flea Flicker TE Delay

TAKE NOTES

BREAK IT DOWN

I believe College Football is slowly moving out of its Spread Offense Era. Sure, we will still see Air Raid and Read Option, but we will also start seeing more Pro Style attacks with larger Personnel Groupings. Even at the FCS Level teams are having success with a Pro Style approach. William & Mary OC Christian Taylor was recently hired by the Buffalo Bills, but before making the jump to the NFL, Taylor ran one of the most efficient offenses in the FCS. William & Mary operated from the Pistol and Under Center with multiple Tight Ends. They relied heavily on Wide Zone & Mid Zone similar to the 49ers or Detroit Lions. One play that became a trend among Pro Style Offenses was the Wide Zone Reverse Flea Flicker with the TE blocking at the Point of Attack before delay releasing on the Wheel. I've seen this on tape from the Lions, the 49ers, the Colts and others, but I wanted to highlight the Pro Style approach happening at the College level as well!

CHECK THE TAPE

Category	SPECIALS
Concept	Flea Flicker
Play	WZ Reverse Flea Flicker TE Delay

Troy - Tackle Throwback

DRAW IT UP

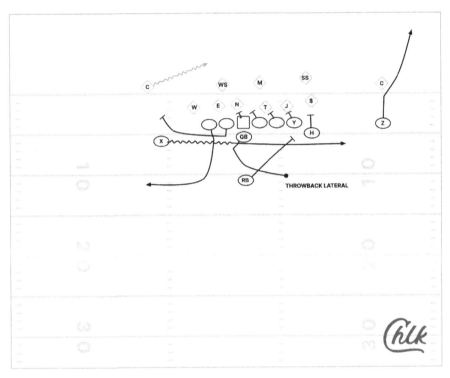

2023 Troy - FUB Rt Razor Tackle Throwback

TAKE NOTES

BREAK IT DOWN

If you are a Football Coach, nothing warms your heart more than a Big Man Touchdown. The greatest joy on a football field is when a Hog gets his hands on the ball and gets in the End Zone. The 2023 Season saw an uptick in Play Callers trying to reward an Offensive Lineman with a Tackle Throwback Screen. During Bowl Season Texas State and Troy made the Sun Belt Conference proud by pulling it off. Formation Unbalanced with the Tight End covered up. Motion the WR across the Formation to run Sprint Out or QB Sweep. The Tackle peels back behind the line of Scrimmage and the QB laterals across the field. This is most effective in the Low Red Zone when defenses are selling out to stop the QB Run Game. Your Offensive Line toils all year in obscurity giving other players opportunities to make plays, make sure you have a reward tucked away in the playbook!

CHECK THE TAPE

Category	SPECIALS
Concept	Tackle Throwback
Play	Unbalanced Tackle Throwback

Arizona State - Polecat Iso Fade

DRAW IT UP

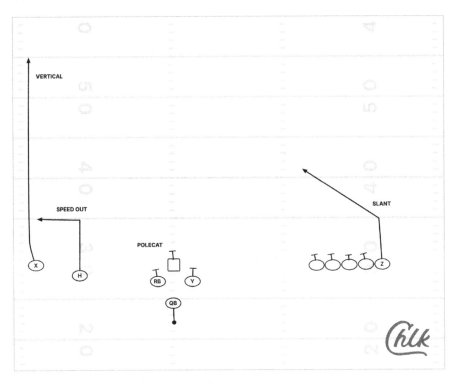

2023 Arizona State - Polecat Iso Fade

TAKE NOTES

TRENDS *in Offensive Football*

BREAK IT DOWN

Kenny Dillingham had a rough first year trying to rebuild Arizona State. It became clear early in the season that the 2023 roster was going to struggle in the stacked PAC-12. The Sun Devils were clearly overmatched when they faced UCLA's vaunted defense. One of the reasons I love Kenny Dillingham is that he will try just about anything to move the football. Arizona State came out in an unusual variation of the Lonesome Polecat Formation. The Core was constructed of a Center, RB, TE and QB. Early in the game, UCLA wasn't quite sure how to match the formation and Arizona was able to manufacture "protection" to take a Shot at an Iso Fade. Dillingham and company pulled off an incredible upset of UCLA and one of the main reasons was because of these funky formations and plays. Sometimes the best thing to do when you're struggling is to think outside the box!

CHECK THE TAPE

Category	SPECIALS
Concept	Polecat
Play	Polecat Iso Fade

Boise State - Snapper Arrow Screen

DRAW IT UP

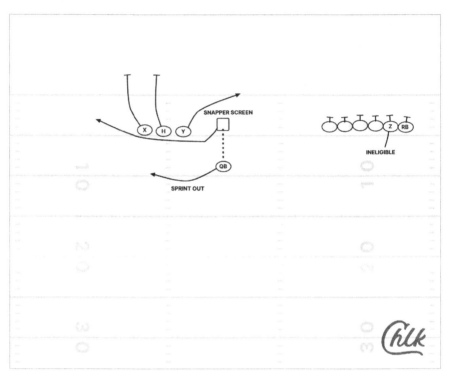

2023 Arizona State - Polecat Iso Fade

TAKE NOTES

BREAK IT DOWN

I have to come clean on this one. The first time I saw this on film from 2023 was when Washington played Tulsa in Week 2. Boise State probably got it from Washington, but I think I've given Kalen DeBoer and the Huskies enough love in "Trends." I honestly could have written an entire book just on DeBoer, Ryan Grubb and the Washington Offense. Boise State did a great job executing this Swinging Gate Snapper Screen. According to the Formation, the Snapper is eligible. On the snap he runs an Arrow Screen behind the three eligibles on the left of the formation. It's a pretty clever 2-Pt Play. Later in the season, Kansas shifted and ran something similar in their upset of Oklahoma—they ended up hitting the Corner Route in the back of the End Zone. The Swinging Gate Snapper Screen was a great trend in 2023!

CHECK THE TAPE

Category	SPECIALS
Concept	Swinging Gate
Play	Swinging Gate Snapper Screen

James Madison - Orbit Return Double Pass

DRAW IT UP

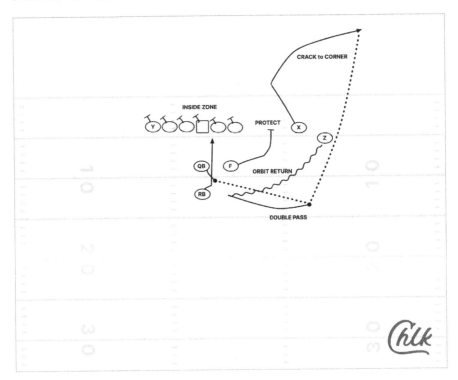

2023 James Madison - Pistol I Rt. Orbit Return Double Pass

TAKE NOTES

TRENDS *in Offensive Football*

BREAK IT DOWN

The Orbit Return Double Pass gained popularity in 2023 as a 2-Pt Play. I sent out this play from James Madison and a month or so later a HS in California used the same play to win a State Championship. The first time I ever saw it was when the Arizona Hotshots of the Alliance of American Football ran it in 2019. While the AAF only had one ill-fated season, plays like this lived on. It's successful because Double Passes are so rarely thrown this close to the Goal Line. The next evolution of this concept might be adding Double Pass capabilities to the 4-Strong Lead Swing we broke down earlier. Keep Stacking Concepts—that's what makes Offensive Football fun!

CHECK THE TAPE

Category	SPECIALS
Concept	Double Pass
Play	Orbit Return Double Pass

WHAT GOES AROUND COMES AROUND

TRENDS

IN OFFENSIVE FOOTBALL

VOL. 01

Made in the USA
Las Vegas, NV
25 June 2024

91424451R00066